Wholeness

Can Come From

Broken Pieces

SaQuota L. Reaves

Divine Healing Publishing

Wholeness Can Come From Broken Pieces

SaQuota L. Reaves

Published by:

Divine Healing Publishing

info@divinehealingpublishing.org

Cover Design: Blair Monique BMo Designs

ISBN: 9781092376013

Printed in USA

Table of Contents

Foreword

Strong willed, confident and driven are a few words to describe my friend SaQuota Reaves. A woman who I know has been gifted with the wisdom and ability to motivate and empower others. She is a source of strength and a breath of life to many. One who can see your brokenness and not be deterred by it but willing to walk with you on your journey to Wholeness.

Often when people would see me, they would say "You have a beautiful smile." I would say to myself, "If you only knew the pain on the inside, you would cry for me." My personal journey to Wholeness is one that I started just last year. I didn't realize that I was broken until God revealed it to me through a dear friend. I immediately took offense to it because I thought, "How could I be broken?" How dare this woman tell me that I need emotional healing! I am a mother, a wife, a mentor, and one that others look to in their time of pain for an answer, for wisdom and for comfort.

After I settled myself and began to reflect on my life, I remembered things that happened to me that changed my perception of people and life. Things that caused me to put up guards and hedges to keep people out and to protect myself. I thought I had it figured out. You stay over there, and I will stay over here. You won't get in, and I won't get hurt.

That was my way of life, my norm. I couldn't and wouldn't allow anyone into my sacred space because the if they got in and got close, conflict would eventually occur because they would see something that they didn't like or I would say something that they didn't like, and they would know the ultimate secret. That I, Antoinette Montgomery, was not perfect!

As memories and emotions surfaced, it was difficult to handle. I experienced a plethora of feelings, anger, embarrassment, disappointment, guilt and more. I asked God to help me through the process. I wanted to experience everything that I needed to experience on this journey. I am grateful to say that I am in a much better place today. I am whole, and I am being made whole. It's a continual process because life is a continuous process.

You may be in a broken state. A state of unforgiveness or maybe even discontentment. You will find in this book tools that can help you start your journey to becoming WHOLE. SaQuota shares her journey to wholeness. She is transparent with her pain during her journey. She takes a direct approach in bringing to our attention the role that we may have played and the roles that we have allowed others to play in our lives that may have us in the broken state that we are in.

SaQuota gets straight and to the point about what it is going to take to get to your desired state. Along with encouraging words, she has included exercises that are going to cause you to bare your soul and own your truth. She speaks of the personal effort required to sift through what may be layers of pain, shame, and hurt that will bring you to a place of solitude and peace.

Get ready for your journey to Wholeness!
Antoinette Montgomery
Founder
Midwife Mentorship Program
"Birthing Passion and Purpose"

Acknowledgments

Where do I begin? There are so many people I would like to thank for their support, but I do not have enough time to write it all down.

First and foremost, I must give honor and thanks to God for EVERYTHING He has done this far in my life. I am in complete awe at how God continues to show up on my behalf. At one point in my life, I felt abandoned by God and didn't know what to do, but like always He showed up at my lowest point and brought me to a place of love and peace.

To my family: thank you for the countless memories. The support that you all have given me is amazing! For so long, I ran away from the lessons I needed to learn through my relationships with you all, but I am happy to have finally gone through that journey. Learning to love and forgive were the best things you all have taught me, and for that, I am grateful! I would not dare name you all, but I will say to my cousins TJ,

Amanda, Amadis (Baldy), Amajaraya, Davon, Karah and Netta you all have challenged me to be great and I wanted you all to know that I love you with everything in me! To my uncles, David, Amadis, Tyrone, Robert, Darrin, and Delton thank you all for your example.

To my aunt, Shanika, Carolyn's baby sister, thank you for being the one that taught me to dream! I watched you at a young age hit goals and milestones that you thought you couldn't reach. I am thankful for your leadership. Every day I ask God to give you a special blessing just because you have always been my She-ro! I love you, Auntie!!!

To my mentors Theresa Harper and Marsha Senior, I owe you both my life. The opportunities that you gave me will always be ingrained in my heart! When others walked out on me, you two pushed me and allowed me to make mistakes, knowing that I would come back to the place you both laid out for me. I promise to keep being great. I love you both.

To Momma Nicole and the Image Initiative, I thank you all for what you did for me 15 years ago! You all were among the first to help move me from my broken state to my current state... wholeness. I love you all for all you've done!

To Herrera, Warboy, Liotta, Barrett, Hahn, Bornot, Sullivan, Boss Lady and Ray, my work buddies, thank you all for helping me grow as an educator! You all are amazing, and I want you to know I appreciate everything you've done for me. Because of your guidance and your ability to lead, SAS is a great place to work!

To the Female Leaders Aiming to Motivate and Empower (FLAME), you all are amazing! You all have taught me the importance of coming to work daily with the mindset to impact your lives. Individually you all mean so much to me, but collectively you all mean so much more. If I had to put it into words, I wouldn't be able to. Just know that I am writing because of your commitment to this wonderful group!

To my Father, thank you for doing the best you could as a father. It took me a while to understand that you could only give me what you had received. I know that life has cheated you, and I am no longer holding the pain you've caused in my youth against you. I love you, young man!!

To my siblings and nieces and nephews, thank you! Thank you for simply being you. We do not spend enough time together, but I love you all so much. I am also writing for you, not only because we carry the same scars, but because we've overcome so much of as well. To all of my nieces and nephews, I love you all with all my entire heart!

To my grandmothers, I love you both so much! I honor you both for your commitment to love me with all your heart. It was you two who showed me how to pray, cook and to keep going no matter what comes my way. Thank you for the lessons and the time you've both spent pouring into me. Lizzie Mae, you are my lifeline, and I want you to know that I will continue to make you proud.

Verona, A.K.A. Sister Verona (LOL), I am not a singer like you, but one thing you've taught me is how to call on God and how to let music take me to a different space. You have shown me how to get up and go to sleep praying, and I am thankful for this foundation.

To the AGENTS, Beejay, Ash, Zeelay and Ja'Nita, I love you all with all that is in me! Thank you for praying for me and standing with me., for reminding me of how far I've come. Thank you for hearing my dreams and waking up to talk to me about the things that God was doing in my life. Y'all just don't know how important you all are to me!

To April, NeNe and Dewayne, simply put, thank you for helping me grow a little more! Your ability to help me travel through those dark times of my life will never be forgotten. You all are amazing, and I honor you all in ways you will never know. Always know that I love and appreciate each of you. Thank you! To the woman that reminds me of my mother in so many ways, thank you for being you. I remember the times I was afraid to be around you (LOL)! Just know that you will always hold a special place in my life. Love you, Ms. Jennifer!

To my Pastor and First Lady, Rickey and Antoinette Montgomery, you are more than just my leaders, you are my spiritual parents, and I am thankful for you both! It has taken me a while to see what you all see in me, but I am finally the young woman that you all told me I could be! Thank you for always being there. Even during those uneasy times, I know you all love me. To Great Grace COGIC, thank you for helping me grow!

To my girls, Ahjelae (Booty), Qui'Essence (Pooh), Niyanda (Niy Baby) and DeAsjia (Booty) and Ti'ahjae (Lil' Booty), I am writing this book to show you that trouble may come, but that you can make it. I am writing to show you the importance of love and commitment to yourself first and others second. Because of your love, I am able to do what I do and be who I am. Being your mentor has been full of ups and downs, but one thing I know is that I cannot wait to see you all make it! Love you!

To Brianna and Ja'Nita (Carolyn's girls), what can I say? My hope for you both is that you read this book thinking about Mom's memory and that you use what I have written in the uncomfortable moments that may come into your lives. It is my hope that you two continue to grow into the beautiful women that you all are destined to be. I write for you! I love you both-- Your sister!

Lette and Tony, thank you both for all you have done. The wisdom that you all have sowed into my life will never be forgotten. The constant reminders to keep dreaming and achieving have helped me reach this point. I love you both!

Lastly, Mom, I am so heartbroken at the fact that you are not here with me physically. I am devastated because 22 wasn't enough time, but I'm excited at the fact that your memory will live on through me. I am thankful for all that you have put into me. What you have given me and how you have helped me gain self-love and confidence is amazing, and I want to honor your legacy. Thank you for never doubting me and for always showing me, even in your death, how to persevere. I miss you daily. I love you so much!

Introduction

Why start and end this book talking about
Wholeness? Honestly, Wholeness is the end result of
this journey that you are getting ready to embark on!
So, starting with the end result produces something
called a Circular Narrative, which just means that
things repeat. Something that is important to note
about Circular Narratives is that when things repeat,
they are not necessarily experienced in the same order
or to the same magnitude as their first appearance. In
other words, Circular Narratives produce something
new. They point us in the direction of hope. They
keep us on the edge of our seats, and they move us
from good to great!

The experiences that come from our individual Circular Narratives don't disqualify us from reaching Wholeness, they equip us with strength, power, love, perseverance, hope, and courage. Before I go any further, let me properly define Wholeness. Webster's Dictionary defines Wholeness as "The condition of being sound in body; the quality or state of being without restriction, exception, or qualification."

Now that I have given you this formal definition of Wholeness, let's now take the time to deal with this term from an experiential definition. Wholeness is simply the state of knowing who you are and being comfortable in the place that God has chosen for you to be. Wholeness is about understanding the very parts of you that you once wished didn't exist. It's about taking off the mask that blinds you from seeing the space that you are currently in and stops your future from shining through.

In this book, Wholeness is taught as an identifier of growth. It's about making tough decisions. Making room for greater things to come. It's about walking away from people, places and things that frustrate your understanding of how you are designed to live.

At this point, I know that many of you are probably thinking, "How am I ever going to be able to become Whole?" You are thinking about at least two or three things that disqualify you from being the person you are supposed to be. Let's break here and do our first exercise. It's very simple. Write down the two or three things, people or places that you BELIEVE disqualify you from being whole.

1. _____

_____

_____

_____

_____

2. _____

   _____

   _____

   _____

   _____

3. _____

   _____

   _____

   _____

   _____

We will revisit these items throughout the book. Now that you have gotten these things off your chest go back and read the first two paragraphs of this introduction and once you're done say these words "I am on a journey to claim, reclaim, discover and rediscover who I am, with the decision that I am going to reach my end, which is Wholeness." Flip the page and let your journey begin!

Dear God,

I cannot believe this affliction has come upon me! I was very careful with everything that I did. I made sure that I said the right things and that I was present even when I wanted to run and hide. I made sure to be consistent, even when I wanted to cry. There were times I thought this pain would never go away. I thought that I would never be able to move past the hurt that now has begun to take over my soul. So I sit, and I wait! Full of anger and uncertainty, but I wait. I pray and I wait. I attend bible study, Sunday morning worship and evening services, but I wait. In silence. In pain. In fear... but I wait. -SaQuota

Chapter 1

Affliction: It's Happening to Me!

The journal entry that you just read was written a few months before I was able to put a "name" to the emotions that I was feeling. This journal entry came at a time when I was having a hard time walking around looking "unbothered." In fact, during this time I was HEATED! I was feeling out of character. Out of line. Knocked off of my feet. I was dealing with an affliction that I thought I would never be able to heal from. That affliction was disappointment.

Before I speak on this affliction, let's pause and deal with a few words that will be used throughout this book; "I feel," "emotions" and "I." I am using these terms because they express the message that I am trying to get you to understand. They take away the pressure of putting blame on other people and cause you and I to look at our past, present, and future situations with "self" as the basis of what is going on in our lives. Using these words do not place blame or fault on our total being, but open up a door for us to look at ourselves and "name" our pain so that we can deal with it.

Oftentimes we have been told, "get out your feelings," "everything isn't about you," and don't operate in your emotions." I would argue that we must deal with our emotions and feelings if we want to move to a place of Wholeness. We must take the time to sort through the things that we are taught to bury. We must not hold onto these emotion-filled events to keep up with societal norms.

The process of Wholeness takes us on a journey where we must call each feeling to life. We must awaken the failed attempts at life. We must shake up the pain that we hide behind our smiles. We must take the time to uncover, unmask and understand the affliction that has come upon us with the knowledge that we might have just opened ourselves up to the thing or things that now cripple us.

Operating in our emotions will move us to a place where we must deal with ourselves in order to improve ourselves. We must trust the affliction. We must get to know the affliction. We must remember how it came to be. We must trace the dark path that led us to the pain so that we can move to a place of healing and love.

The thing about affliction is that it begins in our environment. Most, not all, afflictions start when we are in the womb and grow through something called learned behavior. Womb afflictions are also called generational afflictions. These afflictions can be anything from poverty, sexual violence, mental issues, single-parent households, lack of educational opportunities and work ethic, lack of family support, crime, instability and even pride.

Many of the afflictions listed are out of our control. We are often born into the dysfunction and are left trying to fight our way out of it. We didn't ask for the pain and the pressure. It fell on our shoulders. Maybe you are the oldest, middle child, the only child, adopted, or even considered the black sheep of the family; you must fight the pressure and pain with TRUTH.

The other part of being born into affliction is getting older and learning how to exist and cope with the affliction that was passed down to you. For example, in my family, we are all headstrong. We all have our own way of doing everything, and we want our way to be the way that everyone does "it"! We often argue about cooking, getting together and even about minute and almost unimportant things.

I can see how this way of thinking has been passed down in my family. I know this generational affliction has definitely been passed down to me. One way I learned to cope with this is to take flight. I watched my mother do this for years. Something went wrong, and the first thing that would come out of her mouth was "Let's go Quota. Let me go where I pay rent"! We never dealt with the problem(s) they just lingered. The cycle always continued.

In fact, when my mother died in 2013, I couldn't stand to be around my family. Not because something bad happened, I just didn't know how to exist around them. This time I was alone, and I could tell that they didn't know how to exist around me either. I had learned some pretty good things from my mother, things that helped me in my everyday life, but I had also learned some things that had crippled me.

I can hear you know "What does this have to do with affliction?" I am so glad you asked. The basis for sharing this story is to let you see how our environment plays a huge factor in how we deal with things in our lives, both good and bad. Our environment is one of the first places we feel the pain of affliction. This is why we have to practice something called Sankofa. The Akan people of West Africa coined the term which when broken down means, "San"- to return, "Ko"- to go, "Fa"- to look, to seek and take. Sankofa literally means to, "go back and get it"! Wholeness requires us to GO BACK

AND GET IT! To travel back in time and work through the levels of pain, hurt and disappointment in order to move from good to great!

Now I know that this chapter may be a little heavy and this is its intent. The intent of talking about pain, hurt and disappointment is to get us to a place where speaking becomes second nature. Where sharing becomes an important part of who we are. Oftentimes, we do not speak because we have been burdened with the idea that "you can't share all your business with everyone," but in the same breath we will say "a closed mouth don't get fed"!

Daily we are surrounded by walking contradictions. People that tell us how to live and exist based on the emotions that they often tell us not to operate in. This is foolishness. I believe that we cannot share our testimonies too early and that that we must be selective in how we share them, but I do not believe we must operate in silence.

Let's switch gears here and initiate that process of Sankofa in a broader sense. Let's think of the period of Enslavement and the functioning of the Atlantic Slave Trade. This slave trade was birthed out of the need to label, condition and exploit a group of people for personal gain. The way this trade was able to be born and thrive was through participation from a group that considered themselves superior to another group of people. The subjugated people were descendants from the continent of Africa.

African descendants were displaced or uprooted from the continent to other parts of the world, i.e. the Caribbean, North and South America and more. Once these bodies were taken to other spaces two things happened: first, they were forced to work and live in unstable and unfamiliar circumstances, and second erasure took place, and their minds were transformed. Erasure here means the systematic removal of language, food, customs and the dissolution of cultural and familial ties, often reinforced with the threat of pain, dismemberment and death.

In other words, all the elements cultures need to survive and grow were interrupted and the voids left by their absences filled with pain. The minds of those individuals and their descendants were transformed to see themselves as "other," unimportant and worthless. For many of us, this history continues to affect the environments we live in.

To apply this concept to our various afflictions, we have to understand that the "system of othering" continues to be alive and at work in our lives. We have to recognize that this same system, although its origin is in the creation of America or "The New World," can be applied to those in our lives who are walking contradictions.

Much like our ancestors who had to navigate their environment in silence and fear, people we know today may uproot us and place us in their webs of confusion. They tell us stories of how this and that person said this and that. We listen to those ideas, and we act on them without realizing how their words begin to control us and guide the way we live.

The importance of me mentioning this is that some people will try to silence you because they have not found their own voice. They have not learned how to speak and walk in their own truth. This is why it is important to go back and sort through the afflictions that you are or have experienced so that you can decipher whether this someone else influencing you and your actions or is this *your* own thinking.

Again, let's go back to the process of Sankofa; this time as it applies to *your* situation. Think back to the two or three things, people, or places that you believed disqualified you from being whole. Take one of those items and answer these questions:

1. When did this first begin? How long have you been experiencing this?

_____

_____

_____

_____

_____

_____

_____

_____

2. Who are the people involved? How did they become involved in this?

_____

_____

_____

_____

_____

_____

_____

3. What do you want to be able to do with this?

_____

_____

_____

_____

_____

_____

_____

These questions may be hard to answer depending on which of the items you pick from your list. You do have the ability to change the questions to fit your choice. After you have done this, reflect on the answers and how they have hindered your way of thinking or being.

_____

_____

_____

_____

_____

_____

_____

_____

_____

_____

_____

At the beginning of this chapter, I talked about my recent affliction: disappointment. I did not recognize how long this affliction had been operating in my life until two years ago. It wasn't until I was knocked off my feet by someone I trusted that I was able to name the thing that was bothering me. All I knew was that I was suffering something terrible and I could not find relief.

This was the difference between all the other times I had experienced moments of disappointment; I was able to move quickly through those experiences because I could find relief in other things or people. It was easy to change my behavior towards people whom I hadn't found value in. Since I wasn't wholly invested in or allowed myself to get close to those people, I was able to move past the pain quickly. This kind of thinking was hindering my ability to truly be whole.

What I learned during these last two years is that I had to go back and figure out why this was hindering me and why disappointment was crippling me. I asked myself the first question: When did this begin? How long have I been experiencing this feeling of disappointment? I realized first that I connect disappointment with males, rejection and unexplained breaks. This has been going on since the age of ten.

Second question: Who are the people involved? How did they become involved in this? My affliction with disappointment began with my father. He was the first man to ever reject and disappoint me. My mom participated by trying to medicate the wound by highlighting my strength and by telling me that I needed to push through the pain and show him that I could make something of myself without him. She never told me it was not my fault. So, I walked around with the shame and pain. I realized that my mother was suffering as well due to the relationship that she had with her father. That the advice that she gave me was the thing that she used to ground herself during the times when she missed my grandfather.

Third question: What do I want to be able to do with this? Now that I am aware of how disappointment began and has thrived and survived in my life, I want to be able to sort through the things I have connected with this affliction to move from this limited space to a place of Wholeness.

The move from a limited space to a place of Wholeness is a part of the process that we often miss. Not because we are unaware of the next step, we often want to rush to the end result without going through the entire process. While you go through this process, you will experience moments of sitting and standing. I can hear you now. "Sitting? Standing? You said the next step is moving!" I know, I know. Go with me here for just one moment.

Sitting is often the place where we can think, release and just be still. In a sitting position, we can relax and allow our minds to travel to a variety of places. In a sitting position we give ourselves permission to breathe. In other words, sitting during a portion of this process is a part of revisiting the acknowledgment step that you made a few pages back by answering those three questions. Once you answer those three questions, you are now forced to sit in your truth. You now have to give yourself permission to feel the hurt and pain. You are now in the position to release everything you've bottled up about this person, place or thing.

Sitting is a beautiful space to be in. Let's be clear sitting does not equate to an actual cessation of movement; it equates to the limited ability to move. When you are sitting, you cannot run. Sitting prevents you from taking flight because your posture is off; you are not positioned to run. Sitting is the place where you decide, "Am I going to go through this to see what's on the other side or am I going to skip this part of my journey and just stand." I hope you choose the first option because sitting gives you the momentum to stand. It will allow you to build the burst of energy you'll need to withstand the next portion of your journey. Standing is only appropriate when you have done the groundwork and are ready to walk away from the affliction. We will speak more about this in later chapters.

In order to pull out all of the things that you are experiencing, you must repeat those three questions for each one of the afflictions that you have identified in the introduction. In your journal, I challenge you to spend time searching for the afflictions that you have buried deep within. I can tell you from experience that once I laid all of my afflictions out on the table, I thought I could never become whole. It seemed like there was baggage coming from every angle, but once I had laid out all that baggage, I knew that I had finally taken the first step to learning, and trusting my true authentic self. I knew that the things that were surfacing and resurfacing were issues and afflictions that I needed to fix before they got out of control. I knew that the first step was acknowledging that I was in trouble and was in need of repair.

Let me also say this, this journey that you are on will occur over and over again. The first attempt to get my life together was at the age of 16, and I called that journey "Ugly." That journey was hard and full of pain, but it was necessary. The second journey, I called "Journey to SaQuota." I was 24 at the time; I had lost my mother two years prior, and I survived a nervous breakdown. This third journey, I am calling "Masterpiece." It took place at the age of 26. I can say that this most recent journey has taught me that it is all right to rediscover and reclaim the woman I am intended to be. I know after three journeys that the process is ugly, tainted, and doable. I know that you can do it too! This groundwork takes time. It takes pressure, but I promise it will grow you! Keep reading!

Chapter 2

This is Ugly: Acknowledging the Pain

Recognizing how the affliction(s) have transformed your life will help you change your life. One of the biggest steps towards Wholeness deals with acknowledgment. Acknowledging that you have a problem or multiple problems will help you heal in ways you've never imagined.

The first time I was able to acknowledge the pain in my heart was at the tender age of 18. So much had happened in my life already, but I knew more pain was coming. It was like I could feel the cloud of terror, hurt, and loneliness creeping up on me. During this time, I had realized that the journey I was on was an "ugly" one. It was ugly because I had to force myself to unveil the mask that I had been wearing, to remove the hard exterior that I built to keep certain people out.

The wall that I built around my heart was used as a form of protection. I also used my mouth as a weapon to help protect me from doubters and dream destroyers. Previously, I shared with you that this next stage was ugly; here, I will explain why it was an ugly stage for me. Let me also be clear that although I am referring to my personal experiences, I am sure you can apply some, if not all, of the lessons I learned to your own personal lives.

Having started this first journey at the age of 16, I can say it wasn't always ugly. I had just gone through a hard time in my life, and at this age, I felt that I was better, wiser and ready to conquer the world. So at the young age of 16, I started mentoring the girls that I taught dance to in church. This stage of my life was full of some very high moments. Things were going well in school; I had a job, and I smiled more. I had found my purpose, well a portion of my purpose, and was ready to break out and show the world the new person that I was.

However, one thing I didn't take into consideration in my life before the transformation begun was how the people around me would respond to my change. I didn't understand that although I was changing and getting stronger every day, that people wouldn't necessarily start treating me differently. In fact, it was the total opposite! I realized early on that I had more people against me that those who were riding with me.

So the question became, "how do I stay committed to this new "me" while trying to change the minds of those who didn't believe in me?" For two long years, I decided to operate in this mindset. On the one hand, I wanted people to see the change, but on the other hand, I didn't care if they didn't acknowledge the change I was making. Now as I sit and write this book, I understand that the reason this chapter of my life was so ugly was because I traded in one affliction for another. I moved from dealing with the affliction of "daddy issues" to now operating in "low self-esteem"!

Now I won't say that my self-esteem issues started at the age of 18, but I will say I couldn't acknowledge or speak about low self-esteem until I turned 18. At that moment, I was tired of thinking about what other people said or didn't say about me. I was tired of waking up daily trying to live for everyone else. So, I quit. I stopped teaching dance, and I decided to focus on the ugly part of me.

Before I move on in the story, I want you write about one thing that you had/ have to quit and the reason(s) why you quit doing/ or being that:

_____

_____

_____

_____

_____

_____

_____

_____

_____

_____

_____

_____

_____

_____

_____

_____

Quitting! What is that? How can you live with yourself after quitting? These are some of the questions that filled my mind when I realized what I had done. I questioned myself a lot during this time, and I hated myself for that. I grew up believing that asking questions could lead you to finding out something that you did not want to find the answer to. For some reason though, I wanted to search deep inside to find out why I was quitting.

In this regard, I was quitting because I needed a chance to breathe. An opportunity to be a young college student who enjoyed life as an 18-year-old. I felt burdened by the responsibility that I took on two years prior. I wanted the freedom to mess up. Despite this, I had a hard time staying away from the young girls I mentored. They needed me, and for that, I went back. What I didn't know was that would not be my first time quitting.

Going back was harder than I thought. It was hard because many of the girls did not understand my need to take a break. They assumed that the reason I left was because of them and when I explained that it wasn't, some still felt that they were the cause of my departure. I remember trying to convince them that it wasn't about them. What I didn't realize then was that it wasn't my job to convince them. It was my job to tell them the truth and to allow them to do whatever they needed to do with the truth that I had spoken. I misused and abused myself by feeling like I owed them more than I did.

I know many of you just read that last line and are probably wondering how I could say what I just did. Let me help you out. In speaking truth, it requires us to tread in territory that is unmarked and undamaged. We must go to a place within ourselves that we never knew existed. That place is often our truth or who we truly are. It was my responsibility as a leader and as a human being to say why I dropped the ball, but it was not my responsibility to beat myself up because they could not handle my truth.

I had to learn that the ugly part of this journey was erasing the voices in my head that tried to limit my growth. The ones that made it impossible for me to breathe in their company. I had to do what was best for me, and it took me two years to figure out how unhappy I was in the position that I was in. I now realize that my need to please people had everything to do with my lack of self-esteem. I needed to feel like I needed to feel needed by people in order to feel valuable. I felt that the only way I could be noticed was if I was giving of myself repeatedly. Because of my issues with self-esteem, I kept giving of myself even when I wasn't being shown the same respect and love that I gave. My life literally changed from one affliction to another.

There is something else that I noticed while being in this stage of my life. I noticed that there were so many broken people in my life and the fact that I wanted to change really caused them to become upset with me. The harsh reality is that I was growing and moving to a place that required me to look at everything I had done: both good and bad.

This place required me to think back to the countless times my mom had to remind me that "birds of a feather, flock together"! In other words, I would influence the people around me to change and move in the direction that I was moving in or they would change me, and I would move in the direction that they were going in. Let me put a plugin for you: Listen to wisdom! Had I listened to those lessons on the company that I was keeping, I wouldn't have experienced half of what I did. But since I decided to go on my own path, I experienced much pain at the hands of those "friends" that I thought I could win! I thought I could prove my mother wrong by convincing them to change for the good.

Answer this: How many times have you been told to watch the company you were keeping? How many times have you found yourself being persuaded to do things that you 1) Didn't want to do and 2) You knew that you shouldn't have participated in? I am pretty sure that these short lines cannot hold the thoughts that appear in your mind regarding listening to those who share wisdom with you.

What I can say is that sometimes the people around us cannot accept our change because it would reveal the mask that they too were wearing. Masks are worn to hide things. They allow people to be whoever they want to be while covering up the deep essence of who they truly are. During this stage, I also found out that the mask that I was wearing was used as something called a defense mechanism. I didn't want people to see me hurting. I didn't want people to know that they were winning, that I thought so poorly of myself, that I assumed those around me didn't love or like me. I didn't know the weight of wearing a mask until I had to take it off.

Let's talk about the process of unmasking ourselves. Let me also warn you that this portion of the chapter is going to require you to stand in your authentic self. To block out the voices in your head that try to convince you to not write down the emotions that you are about to vomit up. You need to know that this process of Wholeness requires us to travel to the darkest places in our heart in order to feel the release that we are looking for. Do NOT stand in shame, but sit in expectation. Let's go!

To begin this process, we must first look at the mask or mask(s) that we are wearing. Write them out. Name them. Acknowledge them. Write down the moments that you have to be someone other than who you are. Some examples might be the mask you wear when talking to certain family members, coworkers, bosses, church members, friends, and people who you think may have more than you.

Secondly, I need you to write down what the mask entails. As an example, I'll use family members. One thing that I used to do was wear a mask around my grandmother. I did not tell her the full truth of how I felt about my mom's death. I never told her that I was angry with God, so I pretended like I enjoyed going to church even though I hated going. I would try to be my mother and take on the responsibility that was too heavy for me to carry. I lied to my grandmother to save her.

Thirdly, write down what you notice happening to you while wearing that particular mask. Example: I noticed that I was losing myself and that it pushed me further away from my grandmother. I noticed that I was lying to myself and that was causing me pain that I inflicted upon myself. I noticed that every time I was in her presence, I felt like I didn't know who I was. I felt alone and burdened by the emotions I was fighting to keep inside.

1. When do I feel I have to be someone else?

_____

_____

_____

_____

_____

_____

_____

_____

_____

_____

2. What does wearing these masks entail? Why do I
   wear them?

   _____

   _____

   _____

   _____

   _____

   _____

   _____

   _____

   _____

   _____

3. What is happening to me while I wear these
   different masks?

   _____

   _____

What you have just done is acknowledge the pain that you have been carrying. So how does this have anything to do with the chapter? The fact is, we sometimes work through one layer of pain with the mindset that once we acknowledge that we have a problem we are done. This is far from the truth; acknowledging that something is wrong is only the beginning.

The process sometimes starts and then has to be put on pause when we reach a point where we have to revisit previous pain. The point is that this type of work, moving to Wholeness, stops us from backing away from the truth and forces us to beat through the layers of pain that are controlling our lives. Next up... SHAME!

Chapter 3:

Shame: Why Didn't I See This Coming?

When you acknowledge your pain, oftentimes shame is not far behind. Shame and low self-esteem are twin sisters. When one is present the other is sure to turn up sooner or later. The thing with shame is that it is very subliminal and it shows up in the darkest hour of our lives. When shame shows up, it takes control of our minds and therefore our actions. How you feel inside will eventually show up in your actions. Let's start here.

Oftentimes we do things not fully understanding why we are doing it! Most of the situations we get in we believe will have a good outcome. It is in those moments we end up getting knocked down by a ton of bricks. It is in those moments that we often find out who is for us and who is against us. In those weird moments of confusion and misunderstandings, we search for ways to not repeat the same process that we have been repeating for weeks, months or even years. Somehow, someway we end up right back in those same situations, fighting those same issues. Separating from those same people. Going back to those same people. Somehow, we just can't seem to break free from the agony and confusion.

When we cannot break free from the habits that we constantly indulge in, we cause self-inflicted wounds that last long after the initial incident has passed. This buildup of hurt and pain causes our lives to spiral out of control in ways that we sometimes cannot even see. This is often the place where we learn to build walls around us. We use these walls to lock certain people in and to lock certain people out. We even use this hurt and pain to reject the people and advice that can give us what we need to move past the feelings that are controlling our every move.

I can hear you now saying, "I'm good, it happened, and it's over now," "I don't have time to beg people to stay in my life." These are some of the things that we say to try and avoid the fact that we are wading in pain. We make up so many distorted images in our minds about our current emotionally unhealthy state that we become immune to the things around us. We become full of shame and do not even know it.

So what is shame? I define shame as an act of self-conscious emotion that causes a person to see themselves as worthless, foolish, wrong, exposed and powerless. Shame has nothing to do with others; it has everything to do with us and how we see ourselves. Shame sits right in the pit of our stomach. It is uncomfortable, but we rarely admit how we feel to other people. This, my friend, is a trap. This is why you and I have sat in this pain for so long. We have learned somewhere down the line that all that is happening and has happened to us is solely our fault.

Let's do this: sit down in a chair where your back is sitting straight up. Plant your feet flat on the floor with your hands palms up in a receiving position on your lap. Close your eyes and inhale. Then exhale. Do this two or three times. Try to focus on everything that is currently on your mind. Try to place the individual emotions you feel in separate baskets in your head. Below write how you feel.

_____

_____

_____

_____

_____

_____

_____

_____

_____

_____

_____

_____

_____

_____

_____

_____

_____

_____

_____

_____

_____

———————————————

———————————————

———————————————

———————————————

———————————————

I bet you cannot even find the right words to write. It was difficult. To separate the hurt from the pain. To place disappointment in a different basket away from shame. To try and separate the emotions of distress and disgust from hopelessness and anger. The reason why I had you do this exercise is to show you how our minds work when we do not properly clean out what is in us. If we do not sort through the emotion of shame, we will remain stuck. We will be useless and unable to cope with the things that come into our lives. We will faint if we do not confront the very things that block us from reaching our end result: Wholeness.

Often times we cannot even track how we got to this place of shame. We cannot understand how we started taking in this feeling of self-pity and low self-esteem. Let me help you! You were taught this type of behavior. Sometimes the teaching is direct and comes in the form of people telling you that you would never amount to anything. That you are worthless and will never have the things you desire. Some even told you that you deserved to go through all that you are and have gone through. In other words, some used their mouths to deem you broken and unlovable. The other teaching is subliminal and comes in the form of actions. Sometimes this form of teaching does more damage than the first. How so? Subliminal messages carry the weight of a person's "thought" and this my friend is deadly.

When I was going through my different struggles in loving myself and walking into the purpose and calling on my life, the words that people said to me did hurt and did make me feel less than, but this wasn't what broke me; it only caused me to bend. The brokenness came when I had to face that fact that I cared more about what people thought of me than what they said to me. I use to think like this, "They could say what they want as long as they didn't put their hands on me," there is truth in this, but the bigger issue that I never examined was the fact that the ones who didn't speak out had terrible thoughts about me.

Let me explain what I mean by the word "Terrible." Sometimes the thoughts we have do not line up with the person we present ourselves to be. Sometimes we do not say the things we feel, but the thoughts we harbor about a person can be deadlier than the actual words we want to speak. How so?

The mind is truly a battlefield. This is the place where we store information. The information we store often is categorized upon hearing, feeling or seeing something that we approve or disapprove of. These categories are often based off of our emotional state. Some of the categories that we store information in might be angry, sad, happy, excited, anxious, hurt and the list goes on. Going back to the original thought, what we do not say is deadly because it stunts our growth. When we categorize information, we allow the emotion to consume us in a way that will cause drama, trauma, hurt and pain on ourselves.

Let's do an exercise here. Flip back to chapter one where you picked out at least three places, things or people that you believed disqualified you from being whole and identify one person from that list in your mind. Use the lines below to write a list of emotions you associate with this person.

_____   _____

_____   _____

_____   _____

_____   _____

_____   _____

_____   _____

_____   _____

_____   _____

_____   _____

_____   _____

How many positive emotions did you list about this person?

_____

How many negative emotions did you list about this person?

_____

Now write how you feel about the categories that you have placed this person in.

_____

_____

_____

_____

_____

_____

_____

_____

_____

_____

_____

_____

_____

The purpose of this exercise is to see how our thoughts can be deadly. Now I know I started off by talking about how others thoughts can be deadly.

Why did I present two different perspectives in this chapter? I wanted to drive home the point of how learned behavior shows up in our lives and can be displayed in the form of the emotion shame.

Sometimes the thoughts of others are not spoken, but it is communicated in body language and other modes of communication. I want you to see how important it is to take note of the moments when you go from being the oppressed to the oppressor! Let's flesh this out a bit.

We talked a little about this in chapter one where we talked about the "system of othering." We move from the person being treated poorly or wrong to the one doing the wrong to others when we internalize the things that have been done to us. When we take the lessons of shame and apply them to our lives just as they have been handed to us, we become a part of the problem and not a part of the solution.

I can tell you're probably reading this like "whoa this can happen quickly." Yes, it can! If we are not careful to pay attention to the thoughts and emotions around us, we will become the example that we see. So, the bigger question becomes how do you break free from the bondage of shame? You call it out by its name.

Reread chapter one if you must, but this is the only way. You must make sure that you travel through the spaces that are full of shame and low self-esteem. Dealing with shame is a hard task. If you receive nothing else from this chapter, understand that you can overcome the feelings of shame! You can overcome the thoughts of others and the thoughts of yourself. Take ownership of it all and continue to grow!

Chapter 4:

Faultlessness: It Wasn't My Fault!

L et me let you in on a little secret: it wasn't my fault. Often, we look at all we are going through or have been through, and we look to place blame on ourselves or other people. The need to place blame, I would argue, is also learned behavior. I think it is safe to say that we have all grown up in an environment that may have hindered our growth in some way. I also think it is safe to say that the need to place blame on ourselves or others comes from the desire to have someone pay for the challenges that we face; even if that someone is the person we see in the mirror!

So, why start the chapter off with "It wasn't my fault"? Let me state this first: I am not trying to convince you that everything you have gone through has been someone else's fault or that you did not cause trauma or drama in your own life. I am suggesting that when you move from a place of brokenness to a place of Wholeness, you must look at faultlessness differently. You must remove the shame and need to blame in order to grow.

A part of this challenge is understanding that "It wasn't my fault" simply means I have come to grips with the role(s) I've played in damaging myself and others, and I am acknowledging that often times I did or said things out of the need to place blame on others or myself to release the burden and pain I felt on the inside.

It wasn't my fault serves as a reminder of how we will go from brokenness to Wholeness with the conscious understanding that it could have been our fault. That we could have opened ourselves up to some things that we now realized were no good for us. That we could have damaged some amazing relationships and friendships just because we could not clean out our insides thoroughly to receive and give love.

Let's start here: Love! This four-letter word is one of the most undervalued words used in our vocabulary. We use this word to show our "true" feelings in both positive and negative ways. We also use this four-letter word to discipline and to breakdown those we claim to love.

Growing up, I remember hearing my mom say once or twice that she was telling me things about the company I was keeping as a sign of her love and protection. She wanted me to know that she had my best interests at heart and I missed the lessons she was trying to teach me. I missed them because I was searching for love.

Remember in chapter one I talked about my father and him abandoning me, that's what I was searching for. Some of the young ladies I hung out with were looking for love as well and had the same story as I did, but they looked for love in a different way. We were 12 and 13 years old looking to fill the void we felt from a man who was supposed to love us. They turned to young men, and I felt I needed to buy my friends. I felt that I needed to keep as many people as I could in my circle to prove that I was loved.

Every time I wanted to do something and my friends said they didn't have money, I would split all I had to make sure I didn't have to be alone. That way of thinking followed me to 10th grade when I realized that I was abusing myself by paying people to stay around. When I noticed how damaging it was to repeatedly putting myself in these situations, I stopped.

This was the hardest thing to do. To remove myself to better myself. In those short three years of middle school, I had packed on so much responsibility that I could feel myself slowly giving up! I could feel the burden of denying myself to keep up with them. I cried when it was time to let go! I felt that letting go meant that they would go without. I knew that what I gave to them was what they needed to keep going! What I didn't understand was that I was enabling them to do wrong. I may have cautioned them with my words, but in my actions, I supported their choices! So, I let go, and my life took another turn!

Now I was lonely. I didn't have anyone to really talk to. I was damaged and didn't even recognize the fact that I needed friends more than I thought I did. I realized that they gave me purpose and without them, I felt as if I was nothing. Without them, I was depressed and suicidal. I remember writing a poem and saying that the world didn't need me. That I would be better off gone. I wanted to end it all, but I didn't have the courage to.

I wanted to work through the pain, but my biggest mistake in working through it was not being upfront with my mother or my mentor! I never told a soul I wanted to take my own life! In fact many of my family members, mentors and friends will hear this for the first time. In order to change my life, I relied heavily on God. I prayed, read my bible, and I wrote every day. I wrote about my day and about the changes I would make.

One thing I didn't do was talk about it. That was another mistake I made. I thought I was doing alright. Until the opportunity for me to speak came up. It happened that same 10th-grade year at the 2nd annual Sisters Empowering Sisters Conference. A young lady shared her story about a bully who bullied her for three long years. She talked about how every day she would go home wanting to end her life, said that there were times when she didn't want to come to school because the pressure and pain were too great to handle. She ended her story by saying that the girl in the room told her she was beautiful.

That girl, the bully, was me. I didn't know I possessed that much power to inflict that type of pain on another person! I had become the oppressor! Now here I was starting my groundwork and hearing that put me in a place of shame and hurt all over again. I then blamed myself. After that, I told myself that I deserved everything that happened to me. I began to see myself as a monster. I hid this pain very well.

Why mention this in this chapter? Because this is where my big break came! Although I struggled, I had to fight to see this situation for what it was. I had made a mistake, and I was reaping the consequences of the hurt and pain I showed for years. As I look back now, this vital point actually saved my life. I took a piece of paper and wrote down things that happened to me on one side and things I had done to others on the other side. What I found, was that both sides were equal. They told a story of hurt and pain. I also realized that this paper was where I would begin to clean up my life. So I went through both sides. Item by item. I worked through the list by writing and repeating affirmations to myself.

An affirmation is something that you believe about yourself or another person. Affirmations uplift, empower and inspire! They have the power to change atmospheres and to stop negative energy from consuming us. I also consider these short phrases to be prayers that I send to God when I'm feeling down and out. An affirmation is about personality, accomplishment, and zeal. It isn't about body type or anything material. It comes from the heart and shows up in our being and not just in our private spaces although we say them most of the time in the comfort of our home. To me, affirmations are daily bread; you need it to survive! Let's do this affirmation exercise. Please write something that you dislike about yourself on the lines below. It can be your physical body parts or something that you know you want to change about yourself; mine would be my weight.

_____

_____

_____

_____

Now write a positive affirmation that you can speak daily to help motivate you to either change or love the thing(s) you despise about yourself. Mine would be "you are beautiful, just the way you are! You will make healthier choices to improve your health!" This is longer than most of my affirmations but it affirms me in the body that I'm currently in and motivates and empowers me to make changes to improve my health. It moves me from a place of shame and self-pity to a place of change and motivation!

_____

_____

I spent a lot of time talking about me in this chapter because I wanted you to paint a vivid image of how we can internalize things and then operate in the same manner that we say we are opposed to. I wanted you all to know how easy it can be to blame ourselves and others for what we have experienced.

I know that I also write about somethings being placed upon us in our childhood. These two may seem like oxymorons, but this is just how our lives can be when we do not fully understand what we are going through. When I didn't understand how the issues I talked about in chapter one permeated my life, it became a hard pill to swallow when I had to actually sit and uncover that trauma and hurt piece by piece.

This is also a space where I realized that my life was a walking contradiction. I wanted one thing but behaved in a contrary manner. I said I wanted change, but I kept going to the same places and people that produced the pain that I wanted to get rid of. That in itself is damaging and can produce a web of instability in both the mind and the body. This chapter is mainly about placing blame both with words and actions. As you can see, operating in both words and actions that are not stable can lead us to a life of contradiction and pain. Please know that there is hope and a way of escape. Flip the page and let's talk about forgiveness.

Chapter 5

Forgiveness: It's for Me, not You!

Forgiveness is one of the hardest things to master. The fight to forgive oneself or someone else is vital if one is moving from a place of brokenness to a place of Wholeness. Here's why: forgiveness is often looked at from a very narrow point of view. I've heard people say "it's hard to forgive someone who keeps hurting me. When people lie and misuse me, it does something to me. It causes me to not want to be bothered with them anymore". These points are very valid, and if you're anything like myself, you have said this every time someone has hurt you. In order to understand the importance of forgiveness, let's dissect this statement above.

So, here's the statement again: "It's hard to forgive someone who keeps hurting me. When people lie and misuse me if does something to me. It causes me to not want to be bothered with them anymore". List three things you see wrong with this statement. Be honest if you do not see anything wrong with it and state that. Remember this journey is about being honest with yourself first!

1. _____

_____

_____

_____

_____

_____

_____

_____

2. _____

_____

_____

_____

_____

_____

_____

_____

3. _____

_____

_____

_____

_____

_____

_____

Now I want you to look at your responses closely. Did you mention the role that you played in stopping the person(s) from hurting you? Did you acknowledge that you omitted to set clear boundaries that would prevent you and them from getting hurt or misused? Did you ever stop to think that the things you have been enduring is a carbon copy of how you see yourself?

This is what makes forgiveness difficult. You recognize the first, second and twentieth time someone has misused and lied to you. You see that you deserved better, but for some reason, you never changed *your* behavior. You failed to speak your own truth and to stop the hurt and pain from continuing. In a nutshell, you participated in the heartache and heartbreak. You did not value yourself, and now you're upset!

Let me also say this, your feelings are valid, as are your actions. Even if people don't understand. In order to forgive, you must know who you are and what it is you want for yourself. You set the stage for how all of your "ships' turn out. Yes, it is difficult to channel and control everything that happens in our lives, but I also believe that we can control who we allow to enter into our intimate circle.

Let's go there, to that intimate circle. The word intimate deals with being familiar or to have something in common with someone or something. In a nutshell, not everyone should have access to the intimate parts of you. Let's also mention here that although the term intimacy is commonly used in terms of sexual encounters, I am speaking of the position of friends, family, and mentors who are really close to you. Those who you feel comfortable talking to when you do not know what to do. They are the ones who may also come to you in their moments of desperation.

The best way to decide who belongs in your intimate circle is to look at yourself first and others second. Ask yourself what type of person you are? Are you full of drama? Are you moving in one direction and those around you moving in another? How do you feel when those around you talk about certain subjects that you cannot relate to? These questions will help you sort through your own thoughts and feelings towards others. They will also allow you to assess whether or not you are moving in the direction that you should be going in.

One thing I've learned is that you can do two things when it comes to those you surround yourself with: you can influence them to change, or they can influence you to change. This is why it is crucial to build in personal reflection time. Every Saturday, I take a few moments to reflect on my week. I think about conversations I've had or places I've gone that totally go against who I am and who I am striving to be. I look at the ways I could have done something differently.

I do this because I recognized that when moving from a broken state to a whole state, one of the first things that must be corrected was my language. This meant that my thinking had to change as well. In a nutshell, I moved from being offended to a place of understanding. This also meant that I had to change my perception of everything around me, including my intimate circle.

It is essential to look at your circle and decide who belongs in those spots reserved for people who will push and promote you. Those who will not only tell you when you're right but will stand up to you and say you are wrong. These people will also help you in those moments of error to correct the behavior and support the boundaries that you set in place for yourself. So, what does this have to do with forgiveness? EVERYTHING!

I would argue that a person does not truthfully know forgiveness until they have to forgive someone who they hold in high regards. In the different stages of my journey to Wholeness, I had to forgive a lot of people, and I also had to ask for forgiveness myself. One thing I noticed about forgiveness is that it is a simple process that we all make hard. It is simple in the fact that its sole purpose is to help us recover and advance in life. I know you have heard the famous saying "Forgiveness isn't for them; it's for me!" This statement, although it's cliché, it is very true. Forgiveness allows us to move to a place of freedom and peace. The process to forgive ourselves and others is what makes forgiveness hard.

I've heard people state that they will forgive someone, but won't forget what they did. Out of the same breath, they say they forgive themselves for whatever they've done, and they want to forget the situation even happened. This is a walking contradiction. How can you expect forgiveness to move you to a place of freedom and peace when you create barriers between its intent?

It is dangerous to ask for forgiveness, either in person or in through other means, and then put stipulations on the request. How many times have you said I forgive you, but I won't forget? How many times have you asked for forgiveness and someone said to you I won't forget what you did? How did you feel when they spoke those words? If you are honest, you probably didn't like it at all. Why? It just feels wrong. It feels heavy. So, the question becomes how do we learn to forgive without putting a stipulation on it?

We simply remind ourselves that the aim of forgiveness is to move to a place of freedom and peace. Freedom and peace both require truth and letting go! This is why it is important to acknowledge what you are feeling, thinking and doing. When you acknowledge these things letting go becomes the easy part. Perfect example: flip back to chapter 2. Remember the exercise that you wrote about dealing with uncovering the mask that we wear? Look back at your answers to the three questions and ask yourself this, "How can I forgive myself for not being who I truly am?" Write your thoughts below.

_____

_____

_____

_____

_____

_____

_____

_____

_____

_____

_____

Now ask yourself this question, "How can I forgive those individuals who knew I wasn't being my true self?" Write your thoughts below.

_____

_____

_____

_____

_____

_____

_____

_____

_____

_____

_____

Look back at both of your responses and record the differences in how you chose to forgive yourself versus how you chose to forgive others.

Please do not beat yourself up if you found it easier to forgive one over the other. Truthfully, I had an easier time forgiving others rather than myself. The reason I struggled so much with forgiving myself was because I kept blaming myself for the people who kept walking away from me. I did this without looking at myself and figuring out what was going on with me. I found it easier to forgive others because I was looking for that "sorry." Truthfully, I wanted them to acknowledge that they were wrong and that I wasn't! I needed to be right, even though I felt wrong.

So, that was where I started my forgiveness journey. At that moment right there, where I was broken and unable to accept the fact that I felt I needed people to survive. I knew what it felt like to be lonely. That entire time I couldn't see what was truly hidden in this need to be surrounded by people. Me! I had hidden myself to protect myself, but in all actuality, I hid myself to escape what I couldn't face: me.

So how did I do it? I worked my behind off! I became present! I had to first acknowledge everything that was wrong. This means sorting through years and years of baggage in order to see where to begin my groundwork. For me, it had to do with my absentee father. I sorted through the pain that I tucked deep inside my heart. I had to start there, my heart. I had to work through the feelings that I held deep!

Let's break here. It is said that the heart is the size of an adult fist. My mind was completely blown when I looked down at my balled-up fist. The first thing that came to my mind was: how does this little organ have the ability to affect every part of my body? I also thought about how this little organ has the ability to feel both love and pain at the same time. This thought caused me to wonder how I could possibly tuck all these emotions into this small fist, so I did something that I called A Heart Check!

In order to do this exercise, you will need to grab some paper and a writing utensil. Fold and cut the paper into small sections. On these sections of paper write down the things you carry/ tuck in your heart. Spend about 5 minutes doing this part of the exercise.

An example of some of the things I wrote down were my parents' names, other family members, my job, my church, experiences such as fear of flying, being overweight.

After you've done this, grab each item one by one with one hand. The very first time I did this activity, I packed each piece of paper neatly in my hand using the other hand to make sure my pile was neat and that's when it hit me, this was how I had been operating. I'd been acting as if everything is all pretty and neat when in all actuality everything is a mess. So, I changed the last step in this exercise.

I decided to do some research on the heart and decided that the best way to really figure out how my heart must be feeling was to pick these pieces of paper up with one hand and to also ball each piece of paper up with the same hand. This was difficult, and I ran out of room quickly!

I found out that pieces of paper stuck out of my hand and I watched as my hand had to expand to keep the paper inside. Eventually, my hand exploded, and the paper flew everywhere! This was a visual representation of the status of my heart. I also realized after unfolding the papers that the majority of the things in my heart were bad and connected to brokenness. My emotional state was getting ready to suffer a heart attack! I was living in a sick and unhealthy state, and I knew that the only thing that would help me recover was forgiveness. So, that's what I did through a series of personal exercises.

I want you to know that forgiveness is a choice! It is one worth making. Again, it requires you to be truthful and to let go! Forgiveness promises that you will live a life of freedom and peace once you begin to do your groundwork! Again, it will not be easy at first, but as you move through those little pieces of paper and through the various exercises in this book you will reach Wholeness! Below I am putting a few exercises to help you with this final task in your quest to be whole. Keep working, no matter how many times you must go back to chapter 1, just know you will be whole!

Also, understand this: forgiveness doesn't mean that you are excusing other people's behaviors or that you need to go to the person(s) and tell them that you forgive them. I would argue that sometimes it is important to forgive and move on. I say this because sometimes we can forgive people and if they are not mature enough to receive and have an honest conversation about what went wrong, it can become something that may hinder your growth.

On the flipside, it may be helpful to say something to help move them into a place of growth! I always measure this by looking at the individual and seeing what type of person they are. It is not judging, but it is important to see people for who they are at that moment. Constantly seeing people through the lens of their potential can be harmful to your growth and upward movement to Wholeness.

Also understand this, you will think of those situations again. Forgiveness does not erase what has happened, it simply helps you address future situations and gives you a reminder of how to handle similar situations that if they ever surface again.

Lastly, I would like to mention that forgiveness doesn't mean that you have to allow that person to hold the same spot they once had in your life. It is about making sure you keep healthy boundaries intact and that you work towards rebuilding your relationship in a manner that supports you both equally with the understanding that it may not happen. If it is not possible to rebuild your relationship, you must be comfortable with this fact. You must be able to forgive and let some people go. I am a firm believer that if it is meant to be things will come back around!

Use this time to reflect on your involvement and how you can better yourself. Always remember to forgive with a sincere heart! Keep in mind that Wholeness requires you to move from hurt, pain, bitterness, and frustration to freedom, peace and love!

Exercise #1: A Heart Check[1]

Materials Needed: plain writing paper and a writing utensil.

Instructions:

1. Pass out a few sheets of paper and one writing utensil to every participant.

2. Instruct each participant to write down the various things they hold in their heart. These things can be both negative and positive. A few examples are names of individuals, places, fears, issues, memories.

3. Have each participant tear or cut around the things they hold in their heart.

4. Instruct participants to grab each item one at a time with one hand (strongest hand) and to ball each item up using only that hand. They must keep them in their hand at all times.

---

[1] The following activity instructions are tailored for a group session, but you can, of course, do this activity on your own. Just be sure to record your feelings in your journal.

5. Have participants share how they felt doing this exercise.

The objective of this exercise is to see how damaging it can be to keep things bottled up in our hearts.

Exercise #2: SEE ME!

Materials Needed: Handheld Mirror, journal (paper) and a writing utensil.

Instructions:

1. Give each participant a mirror, a journal (paper) and a writing utensil.

2. Have participants sit in a chair with their backs touching the back of the chair. Their feet should be planted properly on the floor and their hands and laps should be free from devices and or purses.

3. Ask each participant to look into the mirror and jot down what they see on one half of the paper.

4. Ask the participant to circle any negative items on their list.

5. Ask them to write a positive affirmation (something that they believe) to combat the negative items they circled. Remember affirmations deal with inward growth, not materialistic compliments.

6. Have them pick 1-2 affirmations and say them to themselves while looking in the mirror. Have them repeat them a total of 7 times.

7. Have each participant record their thoughts.

8. Have a small or large group discussion of what they learned from this exercise.

The objective of this exercise is to help build positive thoughts towards the things that we dislike about ourselves as a means of helping improve our respect for the differences we have.

Exercise #3: OUCH! That Hurt!

Materials Needed: Journal (paper), writing utensil, and band-aids.

Instructions:

1. Count the number of participants and put enough chairs in a circle to adhere to the number of participants.

2. Give each participant a box of band-aids.

3. The facilitator will begin the exercise by staying a statement, and the participants should open a band-aid and place it on the body part that is hurt by what is being said.

4. The facilitator will then ask participants to share anything that they want from the list of statements spoken.

5. The facilitator will then ask the participants to partner with another participant. Both will stand and face one another and affirm the other while pulling off one band-aid at a time. Ex: You are brave! One band-aid will be removed.

6. The participants will have a chance to state how it felt to have the band-aids removed and how it felt to affirm another person and remove the band-aids.

The objective of this exercise is to show the participants that they are not alone in trying to overcome the obstacles that they have and are facing.

Chapter 6

Wholeness: My Expected End!

So, we have reached the end of this book, but not the end of your journey. You will have to repeat the outlined processes in this book to help you move from your current state to the place you truly belong. Know that this will take time, but you will reach the place you desire as long as you do the groundwork needed to reach that place. So how do you do it? Set boundaries and self-care. These two entities will set you up for success and joy if you do it right.

What is the right way to set boundaries and take care of yourself? To be perfectly honest with you there's no set way to accomplish these things. Throughout this book, I have shared some things about myself that I endured on my own journey. Note that your journey is different from mine, so some things I experienced you may never have to and vice versa. The experiences we have may be different, but the end result will be the same if we follow the process that is outlined in this book. I would argue that the best method of reaching Wholeness is about understanding that this work requires isolation in a way that you would have never expected to ever experience.

This isolation will distinguish your voice from all the other voices you have been listening to. You will be forced to deal with the "YOU" that vomits up every change or mistake that you have ever made in your life. It will challenge you to open your eyes to issues that you never thought you had. Wholeness is the type of work that calls you out of your place of comfort and into a strange land. Here, you will walk the streets of bitterness and healing at the same time.

Walking the streets of bitterness and healing will bring to light the battles that you face silently. These streets are full of chaos and harmony. Some streets are covered in blood, sweat, and tears, others filled with joy and peace. This work towards Wholeness requires a sense of raw and uncut emotion. There will be moments when will you want to and will give up, but you must keep going.

Guidelines for moving into this arena are both simple and complex. To call things out as they are and then to find a solution to them in the same breath is undeniably the most difficult task of moving from being a good person to a great person. This work causes you to speak a language that those around you at your current state of mind, body, and self may not understand.

Let me reassure you that those who are currently surrounding you do one of two things: they will join in the fight to rediscover and reclaim your identity, or they will walk away holding onto a piece of your past. Either way, you must be thankful for whichever position they choose to take. You must be aware that the decision to be whole is not for everyone else, it is simply for you.

Here we have talked about ourselves and those around us. We have talked about the key components that keep us stuck and/ or locked up in a space that we find hard to escape. The work that we have covered is affliction, self-doubt, shame, faultlessness, forgiveness, and Wholeness.

The work that you must do will fall in at least one or more of these categories. You know you are ready and committed to doing this work when you can see yourself in these pages and acknowledge that it is you who is stopping you from living your best life. That it is your actions and your mindset that are preventing you from living the life that God has intended for you to live.

I didn't really talk much about this in the other chapters of the book, but I want to spend some time talking about giving yourself time to process and notice your own change. This is extremely important. When I think back to the times that I started and stopped on my weight loss journey, it wasn't because people couldn't see the change, it was me.

I stopped myself from achieving those goals because I got impatient with the process. I got tripped up on the fact that I couldn't see the change, even though I felt different. I had to assess this behavior that I was exhibiting, and I found out that the issue with changing physically is that I needed a mental change above everything else. Trying to examine the way I thought and responded to myself was a challenge in itself. I was so used to operating in frustration and chaos that I couldn't even understand why I kept failing: my own thoughts.

Let's revisit our talk on setting boundaries and self-care. Simply put, boundaries are a part of self-care. It is about taking care of your mental capacity and moving towards a place of self-healing and love. The question that I always get asked when I talk about setting boundaries is how do you set them? This can be an easy thing to write about, but putting them into practice can be hard.

Start by writing how you want to be treated and what consequences will follow for those who do not follow the boundaries that you set in place. An example of a boundary that I put in place deals with putting me first before everyone else. I had to understand that this does not mean that I do not value other people, but it means that I will not devalue myself to uplift anyone else. If this boundary is violated, I will revisit whatever "ship" I have with the person. After evaluating the extent of our "ship," I will more than likely state that this is the last time that I will allow that person to break code. Next time, I will have to deal with them accordingly, and this is something I will deal with on a situational basis.

List below one boundary that you will set for yourself and the consequences for those who do not abide by the boundary that you set.

Boundary

_____

_____

_____

_____

_____

_____

_____

_____

Consequence(s)

_____

_____

_____

_____

_____

_____

_____

_____

_____

Self-care is an action. It is something that you do in order to improve yourself. Some self-care practices that I participate in are personal dates (Yes, I actually take myself to dinner, movies, shopping and to my favorite spot ever, the Bookstore), getting my hair and nails done, taking a trip to the gym and also just sitting at home relaxing with a candlelit space where

I am reading and writing. Self-care is anything that makes you feel calm and at peace. This could be a challenging thing to do when you are used to providing for others, or you were not taught to take care of yourself in a peaceful and loving manner. Self-care is self-love!

So, to take you full circle here, in the introduction of this book Wholeness was defined as simply the state of knowing who you are and being comfortable in the place that God has chosen you to be. Wholeness is about understanding the very parts of you that you once wished didn't exist. It's about taking off the mask that blinds you from seeing the space that you are currently in and prevents your future the opportunity to shine through.

In a nutshell, your journey to Wholeness has been orchestrated by God. Everything that you have and have experienced was handed to you so that you could get to this place. This place where you are ready to grow and develop into the best person you can be. Here is the time for you to begin the work that will push you to do greater works! Now is the time for you to put everything that you've learned in the pages of this book to work.

Let me remind you that there is no quick fix to go from brokenness to Wholeness. You won't be able to go underneath or over this pain. You must simply go through it. You must face it! You must fight for you! This may be the hardest thing you will ever have to do, but it must be done. Follow these few steps to help you make it to your expected end: Wholeness!

1. Always keep a journal. Use this to sort through all problems and track your happy moments. It's incredible to see how things play out for you. Write about the good and the bad so you can look back and see how much you have grown.

2. Get an accountability partner. Someone who is going to hold you to a higher standard than you hold yourself. Someone who sees your potential and understand that you are working towards a growth goal. They should be trustworthy and someone who you can rely on. They must hold your "stuff" and help you reach your highest success. They must be moving in the same direction as you

3. Pray, fast and keep God first! Always ask for guidance in all that you do. Know who you are and whose you are!

4. Take it one day at a time. The wind will blow, and there will be days when you want to quit and give up... Do not beat yourself up for having those moments. Just do not stay there. Work through those feelings. This is a great time to journal.

5. Last, but not least... Keep pushing! Always!!

Author's Note

My decision to write this book boils down to my decision to repair my life again after another failed attempt to change my attitude and my thoughts towards those who had hurt me. Some situations caused pain that I never experienced before, while others caused familiar hurt. In writing this book, I decided to take my daily journal entries and turn them into this: a masterpiece! This masterpiece is full of emotions, love, hurt, distractions and coping strategies!

In this book, I chose to pour out all that I have within me just to help someone else improve their personal experiences in life! My hope is that every

Queen and King who turns the pages of Wholeness Can Come From Broken Pieces will learn the lessons that I've learned in changing, challenging and upgrading my life! The tears and pain that seep through the pages of this book are followed by moments of sunshine and laughter. Now that you have journeyed through this book I pray that you use the tools here to commit to self-love, self- improvement, and self- care. Continue to revisit this text as often as you like or need to. Here you will be reminded of what it took for you to make changes in your life. Always remember that you matter!

-SaQuota Reaves

About the Author

SaQuota Reaves is a native of Syracuse, NY. She is the founder of Divine Healing, a mentorship, and publishing company. She is a graduate of Syracuse University and Grand Canyon University, where she received degrees in African American Studies, Women's and Gender Studies and Special Education. She is currently teaching English and various electives at Syracuse Academy of Science Charter School.

In her spare time, she enjoys reading, writing and helping other young women of color with issues that most of us can relate to (education, self-esteem, and peer pressure). SaQuota has also received various awards from local and national organizations. SaQuota has a strong passion for writing, Church and her community. She is also focused on helping young people understand that anybody can be somebody, all it takes is a willing mind, a strong spirit, and commitment.

Made in the USA
Columbia, SC
24 September 2019